Nigora Mirzoaliyevna

Big Dreams in a Small Heart

Nigora Mirzoaliyevna

Big Dreams in a Small Heart

JustFiction Edition

Imprint
Any brand names and product names mentioned in this book are subject to trademark, brand or patent protection and are trademarks or registered trademarks of their respective holders. The use of brand names, product names, common names, trade names, product descriptions etc. even without a particular marking in this work is in no way to be construed to mean that such names may be regarded as unrestricted in respect of trademark and brand protection legislation and could thus be used by anyone.

Cover image: www.ingimage.com

Publisher:
JustFiction! Edition
is a trademark of
Dodo Books Indian Ocean Ltd. and OmniScriptum S.R.L publishing group

120 High Road, East Finchley, London, N2 9ED, United Kingdom
Str. Armeneasca 28/1, office 1, Chisinau MD-2012, Republic of Moldova, Europe
Printed at: see last page
ISBN: 978-620-6-74192-3

PREFACE

I consider poetry a spiritual conversation of a person with himself, with people, with nature, with God. When is this conversation necessary? I am sure that when a person is born, a pure image of this world is imprinted in his heart – from parents, Motherland, friends to the Creator, from kindness, love, justice and dignity to faith. If the life he comes across is as beautiful as this pure ideal, he will be happy, if it does not match him, he will suffer. There is a need for a spiritual conversation with someone. He wants to get a balm for the pains born in his heart, answers to his questions, the soul is looking for consolation and sympathy.

The issue of spiritual education is not being discussed today. Literature, art, and music have served this purpose since the beginning of human creation. From "Avesta" and "Ramayana", "Nightmare" and "Kalila and Dimna" to "Gorogly" and "Alpomish", from the ancient literature of the East and West to today's literature, it has been a guarantee of the education of the soul, the freedom and liberation of the soul, and the eternality of sacred feelings.

The door of great opportunities is being opened in the matter of training the great artists of tomorrow. Adoption of a number of decisions aimed at supporting talented young people, allocation of funds for events aimed at bringing out young talents in annual state programs, free publication of books by more than ten young artists every year, establishment of "Palaces of Youth Creativity" in regions and districts, "motherland future", "Zulfiya Award" special attention to the direction of literature is not a small effort.

In addition to these, the literary circles of regional and district newspapers, colleges, lyceums, schools, and lastly, the seminars of young artists regularly held by the Writers' Union should be specially recognized. In these dargahs, we can see that our most devoted poets and writers are engaged in the education of the youth without any fuss or taste.

Rahimjon Rahmat, one of the talented representatives of today's poetry, writes: "Once upon a time, I got rid of the pain of a severe separation by shouting and reciting poetry. At that time, I spent the main part of my day and night, sometimes reading, sometimes moaning and reciting poetry. Then I read the epics "Layli and Majnun" and "Demon". Only the tragedy and pain reflected in these two friends corresponded to the trouble in my heart

A series of philosophical, scientific-psychological and literary works have been created about what the creative process depends on, what kind of phenomenon it is. There are even those who associate it with cosmic communication and extraterrestrials. Let's put aside all the wise thoughts and scientific hypotheses and make a simple reflection – did Navoi write poems and epics without reading many books only when inspiration came, or Tolstoy wrote "War and Did he write "peace"?! In short, is it possible to build a building without a foundation?! Let's take a look at the biography of the poet and writer whose name is mentioned in the world of literature. The creator should at least read the masterpieces of world literature and have a complete idea of the history, present and theory of the literature of his nation. In his commentary on Aristotle's "Poetics", Farobi divides poets into the category of innate poets, ready poets, and those who imitate the verbs of these two classes. Then he says about the third category: "These types... without being aware of the rules of poetic art, follow the sequence of similes and similes. Most of the poets who lose their way and get bored come from this class of poets." Therefore, where there is no reserve of knowledge – just as a nightingale does not come to a barren field without a flower bed – there is no inspiration.

Author

ABOUT THE AUTHOR

Ismailova Nigora Mirzoaliyevna was born on June 7, 2006 in Sariosia District of Surkhandarya region. Currently, she is a student of the 11th grade of the 12th general secondary school in the district. Now she teaches English to the children of her circle in her educational center called "Wisdom educate". Creative works were published in USA, Russia, Kenya, Spain, Germany, Moldova, India magazines.

Member of India's International Organization "All India Council for Foreign Development" and Ambassador to several world organizations.

3

Others:

- "SPSC-(Sustainable Developers and Organizers);
- Global Education Ambassador;
- Active member of "JUNTOS POR LAS LETRAS" Songwriters and Artists Working Group;

- Young volunteer of "OLTIN KANOT" organization;
- Aspiration is a young volunteer of the free volunteering movement;
- Neighborhood coordinator of the "Girls' Voice" Club;
- Member of the "Intellectual Youth" Club;
- Member of the" Let's Rise Together" Club;
- Creatively published in Kazakh, Argentinian and Uzbek anthologies;
- Her creative works have been distributed in numerous nations around the world;
- Envoy on sake of Uzbekistan to a few worldwide organizations;
- "GLOBAL GOODWILL AMBASSADOR 2023";
- IQRA FOUNDATION PEACE AMBASSADOR;
- Glory Future Foundation of Uzbekistan;
- GLOBAL EDUCATION AMBASSADOR;
- Owner of the "Altin Kiran" badge;
- Owner of the badge "Innovative Promoter".

TABLE OF CONTENTS

PROTECT MY FRIEND

In this hard way of life,
Patience endures in the midst of suffering,
May I die in his arms.

GOD PROTECT MY TRUE FRIEND

My glasses are gone, my lonely refuge,
My dear, sweet little girl,
Sufficient for the creator, my painful soul,
God protect my true friend.

I'm the one who opens my heart when I'm sad,
My sky is clear if you are kind,
She is my eternal dream,
God protect my true friend.

She is the only one in the world,
Love is a legend in epics,
Be longing, complete stranger,
God protect my true friend.

Long live my blood friend,
Best wishes my dear friend,
Good luck my friend
God protect my true friend.

MOTHER EARTH

It blooms from light and water,
My heart says the sun is the sky.
Homeland is destiny for man,
People born for the country.

A bridge between two worlds,
A bond of love.
Loyalty to the motherland,
The angel of the country teaches.

Even the spark burns the water,
The world is more or less full.
A person can live a hundred,
But he cannot live without his country.

GREETINGS

Hands on our chests, expressions on our faces,
It is a word they say with a sigh of joy.
We have less place than any nation,
The sweetest word is actually hello.

Uzbek's greeting is special,
Inadvertently playing smiles on faces.
A baby with its tongue out gives full light,
No one is innocent.

Our day starts with "Hello",
There is wisdom in this one word.
Hearts grow younger if they don't get excited.
Jam when there are friends and loved ones.

The moment when he is angry and angry,
It's a strange word when it sounds suddenly.
The world will light up for that person,
Greetings from the heart.

Don't worry about the spoils of the world,
Our life has reached years.
Regardless of the small slander,
Let's say hello slowly.

HOMELAND

The pox that bloomed in the motherland,

It's worth it if you spill it.

The cradle made by the fatherland,

It gives life to your chest and is a great goal.

Homeland will be the sky or a pair of wings,

When you're ready for a trip, you'll catch the bridge,

Homeland is loyalty, great nature,

He will wait for you even if you are gone for seventy years.

The country sings, my poet,

If you sing, the words will flow from your tongue.

Your spirit, your appearance in the flight to the homeland,

If you are fly, it is spring for you...

HEAVEN'S GATE ...

When pains come together and your body dies,

Human heart will skip a beat too.

If your good health fails you,

Your life will be like darkness.

The endless world is too narrow,

You are suspicious of others.

Lek bil, dua is lost without zinhor.

The war that you are making known to ALLAH.

The wisdom hidden in the affairs of fate,

But it is a part of it.

A Muslim should not smoke for no reason,

All this is by ALLAH's permission.

Every great verse is written with pain,

Suspicious love for a heart without pain.

This life does not pass smoothly,

After all, this is the taste.

If your body destroys the darts, this is the case.

Your eyes tear up involuntarily.

On this day, the hospital exit corridor,

It looks like the door of heaven.

THE VALUE OF WOMEN

When your laundry is lying around at home

When loneliness breaks your heart.

When your day ends with stale bread

Then the value of a woman is known!

Have a good night

It's your day if the sun goes out.

If it is not enough, your home

Then the value of a woman is known!

You can try it once when you are a guest

It is difficult if your wife is waiting at home.

Narrow when the wide world comes from longing

Then the value of a woman is known!

Friends will be friends on the street

A woman will be a sweet conversationalist at home

Maybe you will laugh after reading it

Loneliness is a pain in your soul!

Then the value of a woman is known!

Don't be offended, take her heart

I am writing this as a reminder

If it falls on you, it is the day of Suhrob

Then the value of a woman is known!

Maybe this is a joke to you

My forehead skin was shed on this lion

I have one request for men

Hold on to your happiness!

Appreciate your couple halal!

WHAT IS LIFE?

What is life? A grain of sand, but a candle of life.

Sometimes we live a lot, alas, sometimes too little,

We strive to move forward step by step,

Time will be the supreme judge at his doorstep.

What is life? Life is pain or the hands of happiness,

The paths of fate are not always smooth,

To whom pain, to whom sorrow, the hail of truth,

An unsolvable puzzle is the trials of fate.

What is life? Flood stream life is a small anchor,

Who lives richly, who lives here hard for bread,

Some want children, some don't.

There is hope in the midst of pain and suffering.

What is life? Narrow hut, baby, young, old guest,

It is easy for friends and enemies to kill each other.

The price of the most expensive is cheap,

I looked around, as if a lost conscience.

What is life? Between birth and death,
Beshav is the black and white of this life,
The mournful cry of a baby
Behold the thorny border of two worlds.

What is life? Changing seasons winter spring,
Days go by, it rains, it snows,
Don't hurt sick hearts,
Our last destination is only a narrow grave.

FOLLOW THE SUNNAH OF THE MESSENGER OF ALLAH

Luxury - get out of the party,
Leave behind adultery, sin
It is customary for all believers –
Follow the Sunnah of the Messenger of Allah.
Recite daily: say salutations,
Always keep Allah in your heart.
Always return to obedience - faith,
Follow the Sunnah of the Messenger of Allah.
Both the rich and the poor are equal,
Seek refuge only from the Creator.
You will see it in your dreams
Follow the Sunnah of the Messenger of Allah.

May the romantic heart reach these days,

Make pilgrimages to Makkatullah.

Follow the Sunnah of the

Messenger of Allah by truly doing the divine deed.

HOMELAND

The soil where my navel blood fell,

More precious than my life.

Caress – open hug,

You are in my heart – Uzbekistan.

Unblemished fields,

You guys are cute.

Your children we trust

You are in my heart – Uzbekistan.

As a refuge from cancer,

He stayed in Kahraton.

12

He was comforted as a support,

You are in my heart – Uzbekistan.

A land where weddings are connected to weddings,

Don't let your eyes touch your peace.

A proud eagle flying in the sky,

You are in my heart – Uzbekistan.

TO THE SOLDIERS OF OUR COUNTRY

Defender of the Motherland,

Let there be many border guards!

Keeping the homeland peaceful,

Good luck always!

They are there, we are calm,

And the country is prosperous.

Always with soldiers,

People are also peaceful!

A sudden wish for you-

Always go there

Protecting our country

Stay healthy always

13

MOM...

Mother, is your heart so wide?

You listen to everyone's pain,

Is what you saw and forgave equal to them?

You rush and run like the wind.

I give up even if the sufferings make you

You laugh softly without realizing it,

You learned from the lesson of life,

You leave the pain from the heart.

Tell me, do you share your sorrow for once?

You never showed your tears

Someday I will find a solution to your pain,

Let those who don't think about you throw a stone.

Don't worry about the world, my dear,

Don't take someone's word for granted.

Oh, my one and only, precious,

Only you know the eyes of my heart.

You come to life once,

Think of yourself, mother.

We need you every moment

My love is the only one in this world.

I love you more than anyone

Thank you again,

I still take it to Haj,

I wrote a poem for you today!

UZBEKISTAN-UZBEGIM

(QUOTE)

My life, my soul

My princess is my self.

3 thousand century mark,

I am an Uzbek from Uzbekistan!

There are many ignorant people in history,
It's time to bring dust,
From Syrdarya to Amu,
Shokhi Sultan is an Uzbek!

Faith and belief are one,
Man is strong every moment,
With a new outlook,
I am Uzbek by religion!

Many horses in history are stone,
To a tyrant like Genghis,
I bow down and take knowledge,
For Ulugbek,for Bobur.

Looking against the ignorant,
Your loving children,
People call for change.
That's it, my Uzbek!

Faizullo, Behbudi,
He moaned when he reached the blue,
My country is old,
That's it, my Uzbek!

His heart trembled with moaning,

Pamir-u tyanshons,

Tears never stop,

That's it, Uzbegim island!

One of the most ignorant people in history,

Your pain is over

Here is the shokijakhan today,

I am an Uzbek from Uzbekistan!

In history and in the future,

I always have a bright face,

She writes poems for you,

Poet Nigora is an Uzbek!

LIFE

I have many sorrows in the passing world,

I will overcome each one,

I can't say anything in my mouth,

I know what's going on.

There are many people who hurt my heart,

I grind my teeth,

My paper is not full, my grief,

I know what's going on!

If the tests always come one after the other,

I am saddened by the world,

Thank God every moment,

I know what's going on.

I have friends and enemies with me,

I will be together without separating anyone,

Do not tell them what I say in my heart,

I know what's going on!

DAD

Sometimes a single word without saying,

I keep it in my heart.

I have to say that sometime,

Dad, I love you more than anything.

The wings you gave your daughter

I fly like a wind towards my dreams.

You are my only salvation in the world,

Dad, I love you more than anything.

My butterfly youth is flying away

I can see that you are getting old too.

But it's not me, my heart is telling me

Dad, I love you more than anything.

Your life was spent as my child and as my home.

I see wrinkles on my forehead.

Your daughter writes everything in her heart,

Dad, I love you more than anything.

MISSING

This poem is dedicated to my grandmother who died prematurely in 2012....

Open-eyed and dreaming

My grandmother who broke my heart...

My breath barely flew to the sky,

My grandmother who left crying...

It was brought to a point like a dream
The past seven years are painful
Take your favorite red flower,
I haven't been to see you, grandma.

All these years are a sign of you,
You entered my dream last night.
Holding a colorful sheet in my hand,
May your happiness fly in the wide sky.

I spent my childhood with you,
Wearing a red coat and your coat
I would imitate you by being "Grandma"
Now I am very confident...

I wanted you from ancient,
We used to fight each other at every opportunity.
Now you come into my every dream
We used to make peace hand in hand.

I saw you, I froze at that moment
Your lifeless body in the night of darkness.
It's a moment to see you
The only thing left is now, on the day of Mahshar...

LIFE

Who is poor, who is rich,
Who is beautiful, who is the moon.
It is a stream that pleases the heart
Our grave is our destination.

Where? Castle states,
Where? Beautiful estates
Let the rich rich see
Our grave is our destination.

Wealth is our pain,
We do not know our value,
We owe a lot to God,
Our grave is our destination.

An eye that does not see kindness
When he sees it, he cannot recognize it
Maybe the word is a lie
Our grave is our destination.

We are ready for beauty,
We are alone in the world,
We are all one person,
Our grave is our destination.

Otar is from all over the world
One day we will pass.
Wrapped in a white blanket
Let's go to a place.

A DREAM

The skies call to your heart,
Stars adorn the dress of the sky,
Clear color takes over your mind again,
Let's walk through the clouds together.

Let the birds come to us,
The trees are swaying and clapping
A piece of happiness spinning in space,
We will have a beautiful story, a fairy tale.

The sky is a witness to the love of day and night,
Maybe he will tell us everything
We will return safely through space
Maybe we understood the pain of the night.

We had to fly together,
All this is fleeting, a dream
What do dreams mean?
We thought like a young child.

Congratulations to the military...
Always on the go
Protecting his homeland,
How much he suffered,
We welcome the military.

You don't know how your father is doing
Your mother doesn't see you in years,
But never ceases to serve,
We welcome the military.

He does not know hot and cold,
Didn't even celebrate
The friend did not see the light,
We welcome the military.

The mountains are low to them,
Unstoppable pits,

Unable to bring home,
We welcome the military.

Don't look bad,
Prayers be medicine,
We are always with you
Stay healthy.

THANK YOU

There is such a rule in life.

There is blessing where there is patience.

What is the use of complaining?

Learned to live with gratitude.

Your eyes are wet from helplessness.

Few lived in grief.

A person who is not sick is a person.

Learned to live with gratitude.

For your smiling faces.

For your passing days.

For your seeing eyes.

Learned to live with gratitude.

Daggers that pierce your heart.

Don't put the worlds on the cliff.

There are people worse than you.

Learned to live with gratitude.

If you don't find refuge in kulfat.

Don't scream and hit.

Ingratitude is the greatest sin.

Learned to live with gratitude.

Are you tired from suffering?

There is no good friend who is patient with you.

Don't blame fate.

Learned to live with gratitude.

MY TEACHER

I have a song in my heart for you

I will always bow to you, my dear

It's a song that sounds deep in my heart

Don't be lazy in the pursuit of goodness, Master

May life be opened in your mercy

I look like you, the face of the sun

My voice is ready to praise today

Don't be lazy in the pursuit of goodness, Master

Knowledge always shines in your heart

Sometimes he calls us like a light

You are my bright star in the world

Don't be lazy in the pursuit of goodness, Master

24

MOTHER

I'm sorry, my dear daughter

Sometimes I didn't do what you said,

The meaning of my life is only you.

I will give my life for you

Just don't be a patient, dear Mother!

Sometimes you didn't wear it, so that my child could wear it,

Sometimes you didn't fight so that it wouldn't be read,

What did I do to you, at this age?!

Am I a worthy child for you, Mother?!

My paradise in the world, the only one without you!

You gave me a beautiful life

You led to the bright path called Light,

Thank God, you have reached a beautiful age.

God, bless us always,

Insha'Allah, my mother, be in paradise.

My mother says: "You are our flower,

Our aging, beautiful, dark eyes,

Shine a light, my daughter, always our face".

All my wishes blossom in my heart,

My mother is my beating heart in my chest.

Lord, be in prayer to yourself,

You have created great blessings for me

I entrusted my mother to you.

The only one who gave everything for me

I just said Mom instead.

TO MY TEACHER

How many books have been read?

Stretch the rays of excitement from the heart,

Pray, ask God,

If you don't know, listen to your student.

We didn't take your word for it, don't you remember?

We are going to battle today on the field,

If I don't say it, I dream like a mountain in my mouth,

Your words are dear to my heart.

We lied that we didn't make it,

We were just walking and reading,

Call the phone behind the book,

We have never seen the benefits of knowledge.

Increase our knowledge, O Allah,

My dear teacher who taught me this science,

We are the ones who made your hair white,

In the end, we are the ones who justified your trust.

A tale that begins in gold leaves,

Today the cradle ends,

A bright, bright future is on our way,

We will be the mirror of tomorrow.

I AM NOT A HERO

I know I'm not that bad

But what to do, I'm not on your side.

Nothing will change, tear it up –

I'm not the protagonist of your story...

PRAYER OF FATHER AND MOTHER

Parents are the people who deserve the highest honor and respect from their children. There are many verses and hadiths about this. This is the origin of the common wisdom among our people, "Father is pleased - God is pleased." After all, it is said in the hadith that "Paradise is under the feet of mothers."

Every parent throws himself into the grass and water in order for him to grow, grow, and grow up faster, he feeds his child without eating, he dresses his child without properly dressing himself, he washes and combs his hair. "If my child grows up soon, I will forget about my difficulties," he thinks. But the child is often not what the parents think.

A parent's prayer...what better reward is there for a good child? The earnest prayers of parents for long life, happiness, and success of their sons and daughters are endless. There is no doubt that these prayers, uttered from the heart, will come true. After all, a child who honors and respects his parents and makes them happy will receive their sincere prayers. A child who wants to bring joy to the elderly, especially to his father's parents and his parents, is also loyal to his country. Because parents see the respect of their sons and daughters and grandchildren in love for the Motherland. They will never forgive the lack of bread for the country and the country. Yes, in order to receive the blessings of our parents, we need to be worthy of them in every way.

One of the favorite books of our people, "Qabusnoma" contains such wisdom: "A person is like a fruit, parents are like a tree. The better you nurture the tree, the better and sweeter the fruit will be. The more honor and respect you give to your parents, the faster their prayers will be answered." Therefore, it is the duty of every child not to forget the honor of these nobles even for a single moment.

At the same time, receiving the prayers of other elderly people - relatives and strangers - should be the duty of every age. The main way to achieve that dream is to show respect to every elderly parent, don't hesitate to greet them, willingly help them when they have chores, and give them peace of mind with sweet words. "Respect the elderly, don't talk about them in vain, speak politely and modestly in front of them" is advised in "Nightmare". Therefore, one of the conditions for respecting the elderly is to always be polite and humble in front of the elderly, never to talk about them in vain.

I always see the light shining on their faces when I greet them. Their faces will light up and their hearts will light up at the phrase "Assalamu alaykum". "And peace and blessings be upon you, thanks to your parents who brought you up! Always be healthy" - they pray. So many thanks and so many prayers for my one greeting. So, I am glad that this one greeting brought joy to the heart of an old man. I am sorry to witness that some young people do not greet our parents. Sometimes you feel sorry to see those who are blinded by so many prayers, sweet words, and pure wishes.

"Don't buy gold, buy dua, isn't dua golden?" says our wise people. How much happiness it is for a person to receive the blessing of enlightened grandparents.

Darlings! Let's receive the prayers of our parents, all the elderly intellectuals in the neighborhood. It is not surprising that these prayers, made with the light of blessed wishes, bring goodness and happiness to all of us. Therefore, every boy and girl who wants to have a happy life in this world and in the next world should serve and honor these great and noble people for the rest of their lives. May all of us be blessed to do the service of our parents and receive their prayers, thereby gaining God's approval.

Respecting the elderly and receiving their prayers are part of our national values. Because of them, the blessings in the family will increase and Allah Almighty will protect us from various calamities. The Messenger of God, may God's prayers and peace be upon him, said about this: "If there were not among you old men, grazing creatures, and nursing babies, calamities would have flowed down upon you like a flood."

MY FATHER IS MY PRIDE

Parents – this word seems warm and pleasant to everyone. Parents are the greatest happiness for us. We cannot imagine a day without our parents. .Even the nicest things don't taste good.

We should definitely appreciate and respect them. How much they have raised, brought up, and fed us until now. When a child gets sick, parents lose their health. We probably won't live long enough to repay their kindness. Let it be so. Despite this, let's do everything we can for them right now. Because parents are our greatest wealth in life!

A father is a person who can feel the great influence in the family not only in his youth, but also after growing up. Happy is the person who can call his father a loving, caring, demanding, just person.

A father is a strong support for a child, honor, dreams and hopes for the future, the guardian of truth and justice. With social and work activities, with good morals and behavior, Polite is a teacher, mentor, school of generosity and kindness in every good work.

Grandfather Aqil says: "My boys and girls, appreciate your parents from a young age, respect them, respect them, and do not deviate from what they say. Because parents never say bad boy. On the contrary, it is as if he is sacrificing himself so that my child may die in the water, grow up and start a big life. They will make sacrifices for your happiness and future."

Our nation, which knows that "the father is the sun, the mother is the moon", it is the conscientious duty of every man and woman to appreciate, honor, raise them, to justify the salt of the abusive father, and the milk of the loving parent.

UZBEKISTAN - IS A GUEST PEOPLE

Our people, the Uzbek people, have always been hospitable and are very famous among other peoples for their hospitality and openness. There is a wonderful and correct saying of our wise people. It is said like this: "When a guest comes through the door, sustenance comes through the hole", if you really pay attention, when a guest comes to our house, they always have sustenance, sometimes there may be shortages. At such times, when a guest comes to visit, God somehow fills our table. But often we don't pay attention to it.

When it comes to hospitality, I personally think that the Uzbek people are excellent at hospitality. I think that our other brothers do not deny my opinion. Pay attention, we often buy expensive sweets, all kinds of pistachios from stores for guests and hide them somewhere. This means that he will be the first to feed the guest, if not himself. It is impossible not to acknowledge the generosity of our people for this wonderful quality. Of course, someone may have come with a necessary job. The host knows that he is in a hurry. Even so, he offers him a cup of tea. We should be proud of these achievements of our people.

If you have seen someone serving soup for the people in the morning, the person who wants to go to that place can eat a plate of soup and continue on his way. No one will ask you who you are and why you came here. If someone does not want to believe what we say, try it as an experiment. We believe that you yourself will be convinced that our words are correct.

If you go to any region of our republic, you will see the kindness and hospitality of the people. Maybe other nations have such hospitality. But I can confidently say that it must be somewhat difficult to meet such hospitality from another country. As we said above, the Uzbek people are hospitable people. This is one of the achievements of our people and a wonderful feature that makes our people known to the whole world.

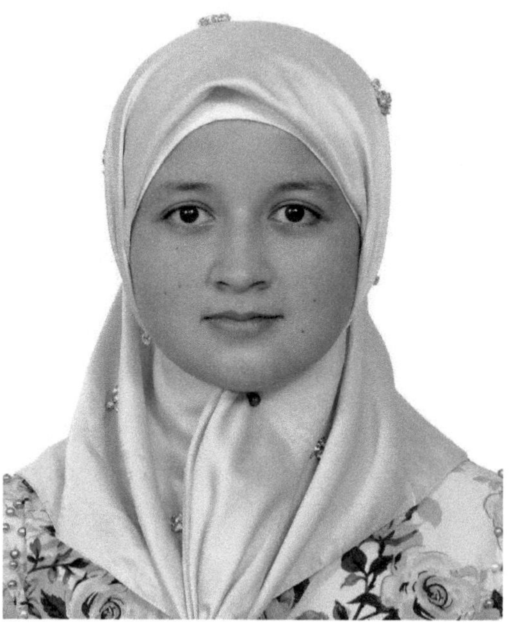

BREAD IS A PRECIOUS BLESSING

Bread is the greatest blessing, Bread is the gift of God's gift to us, Bread is the most loved blessing in our daily life. Bread is the sustenance and miracle given to us by Allah Almighty. Therefore, let us praise Allah for the fullness of our stomachs and give endless thanks. Praise be to God. Thank you, thank you, thank you...

Since ancient times, people have been honoring bread, which is one of the main blessings in their consumption, comparing it to gold, the sun, and life. Bread was spared, hymns were sung in his honor saying that "bread is our sustenance". When a guest arrives, bread is first placed in front of him. Bread is holy. They teach him from childhood to appreciate his honor and not to be proud of it.

10-15 thousand years ago, fire was discovered, and man learned to cook and eat the grains of grain plants, and later to grow grain crops. After grinding the grain between two stones, learning to make flour from the grain and knead the dough and bake it on a heated stone or buried in snow, bread appeared. Many thousands of years later, yeast was discovered, which is used to raise the dough, creating a lot of pores in the bread and making it easier to digest, ovens, ovens, pans, ovens and other baking tools were created. . The first use of puffed dough in ancient Egypt was painting. The art of baking later passed from the Egyptians to the Greeks and Romans.

Bread is dividendi into types such as wheat bread, barley bread, corn bread (mostly bread), rye bread, millet bread, depending on which grain flour it is made from.

We know and appreciate the favorite Uzbek breads that have come down to our time from ancient times. In Uzbek cuisine, there are breads such as obi bread, gijda bread, patir bread, shirmoy bread, depending on the preparation technology. The method of baking bread in the oven is widespread among the Uzbek people. The method of preparing obi bread (which means "watery bread") is very simple: the dough is made by adding wheat flour, yeast and salt. Gijd a breads are made by adding flour, yeast and salt like obi breads, then they are kneaded for a long time and the bread is made thick. Butter and jizza are added to patir breads. Shirmoy bread (which means "bread with milk") is prepared in a special way by adding wheat flour to the broth of peas and fennel, and then kneading wheat flour with milk to make a dough with this yeast.

Dozens of types of obi, gijda, patir and shirmoy breads have been created in different regions of our republic. We call bakers who bake bread.

Sedana or sesame sprinkled on the surface of the bread before closing it in the oven makes it very fragrant.

Currently, bread is mainly produced industrially in large factories and bakeries, and in small bakeries. It is everyone's duty to protect and cherish bread like the apple of an eye.

MY SPOILER IS MY FATHER!

My prize is my father!

In fact, until now, we have said many good things about our mothers, but for some reason we are silent when it comes to our fathers... Why is this? Maybe the Prophet (pbuh) said "to your mother" first??? But alhamdulillah, even though it was late, he remembered that they said "FATHER" for the fourth time...

Dad... You gave me all your love until this day, you encouraged me when I stumbled in life, you showed me the right path, whatever you found, you gave the best to my sister, my brothers, and me first, you always called us with the most beautiful words, our greatest wealth – you taught us how to pray... You were moved to tears by our achievements, you were more concerned about our sorrows than we were. Is it because you yourself grew up without a father, you became the best father and example for us. InshaAllah, it will be like this until the end. Fortunately, may God always protect you for us...

YOU ARE THE BEST FATHER IN THE WORLD TO ME!!!

We have only been proud of you throughout our life, InshaAllah, it will be like this until the end... May God bless our whole family under your leadership.

My love, the mountain that I lean on when I lean on, the mirror of our house, the one who takes a place in the net, who washes away the hard hands with his love, I can walk everywhere with pride and pride, my beloved Father, who always wants to be an example . God, let our life be as long as a maple tree, and let your career be greater than this!

Every time I look like you, my face sparkles with pride and happiness.

Thank you so much for hiding my good and bad and forgiving me. Even if I carry you and my Mother on my head!!!

My father, I always need your prayers, my father, who wished me happiness, loved his family more than himself, may God grant me two worlds of happiness!...

If only all Fathers were like you...

Your girl who sees you more than her life.

Father...

How patient you are... How kind you are... Sometimes I am surprised when I stand. How much God loves me... How kind God is to me. Mashaallah gave me a Father like you. How happy I am... Oh, my father... When you have some kind of greetings at work, at home with a smile, polite and sweet words... I see how many years you haven't bought new clothes for yourself. We only got new clothes for my sister's wedding. At that time, you sent all the dowries that came from the slaves, saying, "Let my daughter be blessed before the gods." I feel like a princess next to you. You are so considerate, so caring, that you are eager to buy 1 pair of shoes for yourself, and how generous you are in fulfilling all our wishes... Heavenly Father, who can teach us to be patient when the time comes... As soon as I call you again and again, I make excuses for the job, postpone it, and run away for the blessing of our family. You are without shelter... You keep laughing at us without realizing that the food is in the place of food... You are so patient... Someone's child is broken. Or if you eat the restlessness, you will be sad like your own child saying "Why didn't the father and mother push him, why did they look at him indifferently?" You give your life to our children... You are so kind, so kind... Having a Father like you is the light that shines on my happiness. To my

Father who does not go... My Father of Mercy, my Faith, who gives up the blessings of the world and prefers our family... .. The days of the Family, passing between the mosques, My Father who is my prey... My Caring Father who taught us to respect each other, My Caring Father who awakened the consequences... Send curses to our house Family-loving Father... If I serve you for a lifetime, if I pray for you, I will never be able to fulfill my rights as a child...

How Good You Are, How Caring...

I love you very much.

My love, my mountain of support, my Father.. If only you knew how much I love you. I praise Allah for giving me birth. Even if I serve you forever, I cannot do you justice. It is not easy for me to write about you. Even if I tell all the people who are in my heart, I will not be satisfied, it seems to be lacking. My love for you is endless. God has supported me so much that he gave me a man like you as a father, I am very happy, Alhamdulillah. You are the Fortress of our family. We rely on you. The stronger you are, the more confident we are, the stronger we feel. May God give you long life. As a father loves his child, so you love me. You support me more than all the Fathers in the world. That's why I always feel like a Princess.

My father, you are so kind and caring that even a small thorn will kill you, you will lose your happiness. Even if you have a lot of work, you make time for me and call me all day long to ask how I am. How kind you are, my Father.

What am I spending my time on, am I focusing my life on meaningful and useful things? My family-loving father, who asks these questions every day. What kind of person would I be if you weren't so strict. My Father, who always scolds me thinkning about tomorrow. I will not be disappointed with them at all. I know you wish me well. I am pleased to advise you, Father.

I remember that you are kind to my grandfather and grandmother. You are so considerate that you would do anything for them. May God's places be from heaven. I'm thinking. Can I be a child like you? Can I laugh like you and be kind like you? I don't know.. But I will say that until the end of my life I will do all the good that I can, InShaAllah

You always say that you love us more, but I'm just not sure how that can be true. Love you a million times over, dad.When it comes to dads, I don't think it could get any better than this. Celebrating you today reminds me just how much you touch those around you!

God took the strength of a mountain, the patience of eternity, and combined them to create the thing we call dad.

To my dad, the man who moves fire and earth for his family.

All of the lessons you've taught me over the years have added up to the wonderful life I'm living today.Love begins and ends with a father.

A dad's job isn't about being everything to everyone. Just everything to someone.

Every dad is special. Just not as special as you.

As it turns out, he was the best dad ever. The end.

When I count my blessings, I start with you.

MY MOTHER IS MY HEAVEN

My mother is a symbol of honesty, love and sincerity for me. My mother is always praying. Mom is ready to give us everything, but does not ask for anything in return. Mother's care for each of us in our family encourages me to do the same in the future.

Although my mother is not physically strong, she is able to overcome any obstacles for her life and family. He encourages me to be like that and never gives up when times are tough. Most importantly, my mother encourages me to be thorough in every way and to learn. My favorite words of my mother: "Don't try again and again until you succeed, my child, every time you start with the experience you got from the previous failure."

When I'm not having a good day or when I hear something from my dad, I always run to my mom because she saves me from any problems. Whether it's a small homework or a big problem, she's always there for me.

If I was afraid of the dark, he would become my light and save me from that darkness. Also, if I couldn't sleep at night, she would hold my head on her lap until I fell asleep.

My mother is not ordinary, she is my superhero. She supports and encourages me every step of the way. I am always by my side, regardless of the circumstances, day or night. In addition, his every work, determination, loyalty, selflessness, behavior inspire me.

I love my mother. We must respect our elders. But I respect my mother in a completely different way, she took care of me even when I could not speak and walk. My mother is the only one who understood me what I want through one collection.

In addition, my mother taught me to walk, talk and take care of myself. Similarly, every big step I have taken in my life is all because of my mother. Because if my mother had not taught me to take small steps, I would not have been able to take this big step.

Every mother is a special person for her children. He is a wonderful teacher, a dear friend, a strict teacher. If there is a person who loves us more than our mother, it is only Allah. Not only my mother, but every mother who sacrifices her life for her family deserves praise and applause.

Thanks to our mothers, we learned to read and write, to solve all kinds of problems encountered in life... We learned to distinguish between good and bad, and we ourselves were able to treat the people around us well. My mother taught me to appreciate life and every moment. He taught us to be hardworking and responsible people. My mother taught us to value people, to take care of loved ones, not to hurt children and to respect adults.

Being a mother is a profession, unfortunately, not everyone appreciates it. Can a woman be called a mother who gave birth and abandoned her child, or worse, trashed it? Can a woman be called a real mother if instead of buying something for her baby, she only tries to please herself, get drunk and scold her child? Does a person who constantly mocks, beats and abuses a child even for the most innocent offense deserve the honorary title of MOTHER? Can we call a real mother who puts happiness and well-being above the happiness of her child? Does this woman deserve to be a mother if she allows others to make fun of her little man? No. A real mother will never betray, deceive, substitute or hurt her baby, she will never value her freedom more than her child. A real mother always protects her child and does not harm anyone. This is a real, loving and caring mother.

It is such kind, honest, loving, caring and sincere mothers that you should idolize them. Such mothers should be prayed for every day, every hour and every second.

THE LAND OF GREAT SCHOLARS

Our land has always been the land of great scholars, thinkers, and geniuses who were ahead of their time. Abu Rayhan Beruni, Ahmed Fargani, Mirza Ulug'bek, Ali Qushchi, Alisher Navai, Abu Ali ibn Sina, Mahmud Zamakhshari, Abu Bakr Qaffol Shoshi, Abu Mansur Moturidi, Abdukhalik G'ijduvani, Bahauddin Naqshband, Abulmuin Nasafi, Burhoniddin Marginani, Imam Bukhari, Imam Termizi, Imam Dorimi... the names of them are a book. One is a master of the science of theology, one is a great scientist who put a ladder to the sky, another is the father of applied medicine, one is a master of the science of theology, and another is the sultan of scholars.

Imam Muhammad ibn Ismail al-Bukhari is undoubtedly one of our great ancestors who deserves special respect and attention in the Islamic world, and who gives us pride in Muslim countries. His achievements in the path of knowledge, his contributions to the development of the science of hadith, and his works have become legends in many languages throughout the world. The collection of hadiths "al-Jame' as-sahih", which is the first sacred source of Islam, after the Holy Qur'an, is also a testament to the great scholar's many years of scientific activities and his dedication to the Islamic community. It is a product of biased approaches. A lot can be said about Imam Bukhari, a lot has been said and will be said in the future. After all, in the conditions of the Middle Ages, it is a great service and honor that no one is given, even in today's age of technology and wide opportunities, to write down about a million hadiths from thousands of narrators scattered around the world, one by one, checking and classifying books. About 7,500 hadiths that this great muhaddith had memorized with their narrators and isnads, and his book "al-Jame' as-sahih" is considered the most reliable collection of hadiths in the Islamic world.It is known that today in our country great attention is paid to the religious and educational sphere, various educational institutions and centers are being established in order to educate young people to become a generation worthy of our ancestors, and great work is being done in this regard. Deeply studying the unique legacy of our great scholars who made a great contribution to the Islamic religion on a scientific basis, widely promoting among our compatriots and the international community that the soil of our holy land has been the homeland of great scholars and dear saints since time immemorial, national- preserving and developing our religious values, on this basis educating the young generation in the spirit of good ideas, strengthening the feeling of love and loyalty to the Motherland in their hearts has become our main idea. No matter where the honorable President goes, no matter where he is in our country, he will restore the name and legacy of the saints, scientists and thinkers who were born and raised there, beautify the places where they settled forever, and establish various places of interest named after them. They are personally taking the initiative in the work of defining the scope of their activities in a wide and precise manner.

SCHOOL IS A GRAT INSTITUTION

A school is an educational institution where the young generation is informed and educational activities are carried out under the guidance of a teacher.

School is a sacred place where human perfection is formed. There is a person who, when he steps on the threshold of school, remembers his most innocent, most sincere, most beautiful times. The main task of us pedagogues is to educate and raise our children who are educated, who create the future, who believe in our country, who glorify the glory of our land.

School is the holy place that brought big dreams, lofty goals and aspirations to my little heart for the first time. School is the place where I aspire every morning.

School is the place where I found my kind teacher who taught me to write with a pencil for the first time and took me into his unique magical world.

The importance of the school in bringing out every talent and ability, showing the appropriate path to the student aspirations is huge.

After the Republic of Uzbekistan gained independence, a number of works were carried out in the field of developing the material and technical base of schools, providing them with scientific methods. School work is developing rapidly in Uzbekistan.

If we look at the history of the developed countries of the world, we can see that the reforms aimed at changing the life of the society started with the education system, kindergarten, school, education. Because it is impossible to change a person and society without changing the school. The foundation of education and upbringing is the school. Teachers are the force that makes a school a school.

From the first days of his presidency, the President of the Republic of Uzbekistan, Shavkat Mirziyoyev, has been paying special attention to the issues of training innovative and creatively thinking, modern personnel in our country, educating young people in the spirit of patriotism and high spirituality, and for this purpose, improving the education system.

The issue of raising the young generation with high morals and spirituality, and teaching them the most modern knowledge and skills is considered a priority by the President. According to the will of our people, parents, pedagogical team and students, the 11-year education system was introduced in our country. This is the main factor in properly organizing the free time of young people, ensuring that they are constantly under the eyes of their parents and teachers, and acquiring knowledge thoroughly and without distraction. At the same time, in order to further improve the quality of educational work, attention to pedagogues has been increased more than ever. Along with knowledge, young people are deeply instilled in the school with the lessons of humanity, honest work for the development of the Motherland, and the skills to use the blessings of independence as the apple of an eye.

President of the Republic of Uzbekistan Shavkat Mirziyoyev chaired a meeting of video selectors dedicated to the issues of developing the public education system, increasing the qualifications and influence of pedagogues in society, and raising the morale of the young generation.

However, despite the positive changes being implemented, there are still systemic problems in the education system, the material and technical base of schools, and the knowledge and skills of some teaching staff do not meet the requirements of today's time.

The need to create a modern and rational system in the field of education, to update teaching methods, educational Standarts, textbooks and training manuals, to use best foreign experiences in education, and to use national traditions and the importance of relying on values was noted.

The head of our state emphasized the importance of carefully developing the national idea and its ideological foundations, and educating the young generation in the spirit of national pride and patriotism, based on the principle "From national revival to national progress."

Particular attention was paid to the need for the participation of parents and the general public in order to correct deficiencies in schools and control the quality of education.

Therefore, we wish the teachers to be diligent in this way, not to get tired in cultivating personnel who will be real children of our ancestors and continue their path.

EDUCATION IS THE BASIS OF ALL KNOWLEDGE

The word education contains various concepts. Knowledge, intelligence, understanding, perception, perception, wisdom, sophistication, experience, knowledge are among them.

Education is the basis of all knowledge. There is a lot of information in this single word. Because an uneducated person does not have the ability to be creative and see the wonders of the world. Human mind can only be developed by education. The heart and soul are connected to the heights. Enjoys spirituality and enlightenment.

Processes aimed at the formation of physical, mental, moral and spiritual qualities in every person constitute education.

Education not only shows the worldview, spiritual and moral level, Morality and Aesthetics of individuals. On the contrary, it determines his ideas, thoughts, mobility, everything in social life. The universe is embodied under the concept of education. Education is a mirror that reveals the spiritual and moral image of a person. Only education has a decisive importance not only in the life of some people, but in the life of the whole society and country. As a result of not paying enough attention to the education of the representatives of future generations and society members in general, and many neglects, the life of the country is undergoing radical changes.

As a result of the violation of moral norms, instead of development, crises increase in the society, especially the uneducated activities of young people change the fate of the whole society. In order to prevent them, it is necessary to place the ideas of national education in the child's mind from a young age, to warn about the mistakes and deficiencies caused by the lack of education, and to explain the consequences. Actions taken without thinking about the consequences will be bad. The starting point of every work is done with discipline and discipline. Because if children are taught the concept of education from a young age, mistakes related to education will not be made in the future. Indiscipline, violations, crimes and disorder are absolutely not allowed. As a result, such problems are reduced.

"Another important issue that we always have in mind is the morality, behavior, and world view of our youth. Nowadays, times are changing rapidly. Young people feel these changes the most!

Be in harmony with the demands of youth. But at the same time, remember that you are small. May the call of who we are and the descendants of great men always echo in their hearts and encourage them to remain faithful to their beliefs. How can we do this?

At the expense of education, education and only education."

These words were expressed by President Shavkat Mirziyoyev as a reminder to the youth of Uzbekistan.

The President calls on the young generation to be well-informed, educated, knowledgeable and clear. Everyone is responsible for their future.

For this reason, it is the responsibility of every parent to raise their children as healthy individuals. Raising healthy, well-educated, educated, intelligent children is difficult only with the upbringing of parents. If the neighborhood is like mother and father's child, the people who have a say in the environment should also get used to such actions. That's when we set an example for adults and children and share what we want. Children who develop their country and society grow up.

Kindergartens and schools interested in children's education are increasing. First of all, the teachers teaching the child should be qualified, educated and experienced. Because where there is education, the conditions of education are also excellent. Today, in the age of advanced technology, time is moving fast. Modern information technologies solve people's problems.

Therefore, it is necessary and necessary to make our children interested in books from a young age.

Knowledge and education are an inseparable whole. The book is actually a tool for children to understand these feelings...

JO`NALISH
KELISHIGI

O`RIN- PAYT
KELISHIGI

CHIQISH
KELISHIGI

"I AM PROUD TO BE AN UZBEK GIRL"

In Uzbekistan, the necessary conditions and opportunities have been created for the healthy and well-rounded education of young people, the realization of their creative and intellectual potential, and the development of them as well-rounded individuals. Long-term personnel training, nationwide programs for the development of school education, state policy on youth, state awards established for our sons and daughters in various fields, structured education facilities, activities related to the development of children's sports. All these are part of the activities aimed at raising a mature generation, that is, the worthy successors of our tomorrow, the enthusiasts of the country's future.

It is gratifying to realize the above noble idea and goals - to educate young people in the spirit of loyalty and love for the motherland, respect for national and universal values, and in the spirit of patriotism, to realize the dreams of our sons and daughters. we can see today's aspirations in every field on all fronts.

In fact, each of us is responsible for young people to have an independent outlook and an active life position. The goal is ours only if we manage to educate their spiritual and moral qualities, to live with a sense of patriotism, responsibility for the fate of the country, to strengthen the sense of strengthening the independence of our country, and to make our sons and daughters educated in all aspects. It is necessary to inculcate in the minds of young people about the great potential of our country, spiritual-educational, socio-economic opportunities, the ancient and rich history of our country, the great contribution of our great ancestors and the cultural heritage left by them to the culture and development of mankind. . As we are mobilizing all our strength and capabilities so that our nation is not inferior to anyone else in the world, and our children live stronger, more educated, wiser and of course happier than us, in this regard, the issue of spiritual education is undoubtedly of incomparable importance. is enough. If we lose our vigilance and sensitivity, determination and responsibility in this matter, if we leave this very important work to its own devices, if we lose our sacred values. and we may lose our spirituality and historical memory fed by them, and in the end, we may deviate from the path of universal development that we aspire to."

If we look at the history, Oychechak, who gave birth to a boy as brave as Jalaliddin 800 years ago, was able to infuse the breath of her country, love, and great longing for freedom into the blood of her children along with breast milk. He raised his son and daughter in the spirit of devotion to the Motherland and love for the people. Jalaliddin's life, which ended tragically, was recorded in the pages of history as an unparalleled example of courage. He went to save his sister, who was captured by the Persians in Isfandiyar Khazar country, and he himself was captured. "What do you want?" was asked. And he said, "A pinch of soil and a sip of water of my country."

Yes, in the heart of every person there should be love for the place of birth. A philosopher was asked: "How do you endure this desert wilderness, where it is difficult to live?" He answered: "If a person did not have love for his birthplace, there would not be enough people in prosperous cities."

If we turn the pages of the glorious history of our beloved country, we will witness the patriotism of our ancestors. The leader of the great sect, Najmuddin Kubro, set an example of great patriotism in the history of our country. He did not listen to any wishes other than the wishes of his love for the country. The courage of patriotic children is eternal. Peace in general depends on sustainable development.

HUMILITY

When we talk about humility, we sometimes think of a gullible, simple, shy person. But this kind of imagination is not right, just as everything is not right before our eyes. To know what real humility is, you need to look for its antonym. Undoubtedly, it is selfishness, arrogance and conceit. So, what makes arrogance and conceit? In our opinion, he sees the blessing given by God as a blessing of his own creation, and it comes from ignorant pride and ignorance of the original owner and creator of the blessing.

A humble person is always satisfied and grateful for every blessing. A humble person has impartiality in everything he does. Let's say that even if he helps a person in a difficult situation, he does not give him anything in return. No matter what field a humble person works in, he will certainly find respect and value in that place. He does not need to introduce himself to the world, people will quickly find him. Because this person with modest virtue is a necessary person at all times and in all places. That is why our Prophet Muhammad, may

God's prayers and peace be upon him, said in one of his hadiths: "The best of worship is humility, that is, humility."

Hazrat Abdukholiq G'ijduvani writes: "If your heart wants to talk, talk to the poor, the broken-hearted, and the people of God." If you want to be famous, don't be famous. Don't order someone to serve you. Carry your own burden. Humble yourself always, everywhere. It is a very important quality to consider yourself inferior to others. Look at all of God's creatures, big and small, with kindness and compassion. Don't know them at all..." they wrote.

Humility means good intentions, humanity, tact, generosity, knowing honor, valuing friends and others in general, being able to respect, spiritual purity...

In the etiquette of folk art, the benefits of modesty and the harmful consequences of arrogance, which is considered a flaw for a person, are fully reflected through life events and instructive images.

People who wear humility are the best and most honest people in life. They do not allow arrogance, pomposity, exaggeration, exaggeration, and lying.

Pride is a sign of insanity. Arrogance and pride destroy a person. Proud people are subject to the wrath of society. Although proud and arrogant people are rich, scientists, and officials, they do not have any prestige or value in society. Their true friends are inexhaustible, and those who have them do not lose them when a bad day befalls them. In the end, they are condemned to live in humiliation and loneliness.

FLOWERS ARE A SYMBOL OF DELICITY

Flowers, flowers! Flowers accompany us throughout our lives: they welcome us at birth, comfort us in old age, cheer us up at weddings, days and holidays, and come on unforgettable dates. Flowers are needed both at home and at work, in spring and severe cold, in hot summer and autumn, life is poor without their beauty. Flowers reveal to a person the possibility to know beauty, to feel the fullness of life. Being close to flowers and thinking about their unique beauty softens the heart and reveals the best aspects of human character.

"To live, you need sun, freedom and a small flower," said the great storyteller Hans Christian Andersen. The world of flowers is mysterious and wonderful. Thousands of their species still decorate our planet and are the brightest manifestation of love. And many flowers in our forests are included in the Red Book, an alarming list of protected plants. But if people do not realize that without flowers, forests and greenery, the ban itself will do nothing By conserving nature, we protect the health and well-being of those who come for us.

Today we are preparing to write an essay on "Flowers – beauty, flowers – life". Let's dive into the world of beauty. And one must agree with the words of Cervantes. "Beauty has the power and gift to bring peace to the soul."

In a world full of technology and concrete, flowers are a breath of nature that brings us back to the simple beauty of life. They are not only a beauty for the eyes but also a blessing for the soul. The importance of flowers is often overlooked, but they play a crucial role in our lives, from improving mood and health to enhancing human relationships and culture.

The first and most obvious benefit of flowers is their positive effect on mood. Even a single flower can make a huge difference to a room or someone's life. They can be used to bring light and color to a dark place or to provide a sense of calm and relaxation in a crowded place. Some flowers have a calming or energizing effect, so they can be used to improve sleep or increase energy.

Flowers certainly bring a touch of color and beauty to our lives. These are not only plants, but have a deeper meaning, often associated with feelings and emotions. Flowers can be a great gift to show someone you appreciate them or to bring a sense of optimism into their life. Flowers can also be used to decorate various events such as weddings, christenings or other celebrations, they bring elegance and romance.

Flowers have always been considered a symbol of beauty, tenderness and love. They can improve the appearance of the garden or the interior, but in addition to the aesthetic appearance, they also have an ecological value. Flowers are an integral part of the ecosystem and are important for plant pollination, biodiversity and ecological balance.

Flowers are important in many aspects of our life. They are essential to the natural environment, add color and beauty to art and culture, are used in the food industry, and have healing properties. It is important to recognize the importance of these natural beauties and to use and enjoy them responsibly.

Printed by Books on Demand GmbH, Norderstedt / Germany